WOLVERINES

LIVING WILD

Published by Creative Education
P.O. Box 227, Mankato, Minnesota 56002
Creative Education is an imprint of The Creative Company
www.thecreativecompany.us

Design and production by Mary Herrmann
Art direction by Rita Marshall
Printed in the United States of America

Photographs by Alamy (Dylan Becksholt, Design Pics Inc., Juniors Bildarchiv GmbH, John Lens, tbkmedia.de), Dreamstime (Lukas Blazek, Emanuel Corso, Moose Henderson, Caroline Henri, Richard Lowthian, Jamen Percy, Howard Sandler, Tt), iStockphoto (mb-fotos, photos_martYmage), Shutterstock (BMJ, Tom Burlison, DiscoDad, dotweb Steen B Nielsen, Andreas Gradin, Marc Herrmann, Vitaly Ilyasov, Justin Kral, Torsten Lorenz, Erik Mandre, Scott E Read, Rruntsch, slava17), SuperStock (Biosphoto, Frans Lemmens, Minden Pictures), Wikipedia (Johnbod, Marcusroos, Wikimedia)

Library of Congress Cataloging-in-Publication Data
Gish, Melissa.
Wolverines / Melissa Gish.
p. cm. — (Living wild)
Includes bibliographical references and index.
Summary: A scientific look at wolverines, including their habitats, physical characteristics such as their claws, behaviors, relationships with humans, and limited range of the hungry weasels in the world today.
ISBN 978-1-60818-421-7
1. Wolverine—Juvenile literature. I. Title. II. Series: Living wild.

QL737.C25G58 2014
599.76'6—dc23   2013031809

CCSS: RI.5.1, 2, 3, 8; RST.6-8.1, 2, 5, 6, 8; RH.6-8.3, 4, 5, 6, 7, 8

First Edition
9 8 7 6 5 4 3 2 1

CREATIVE EDUCATION

WOLVERINES

Melissa Gish

In Montana's Gallatin National Forest, a wolverine treads a deer path, moving silently over a thick carpet of ponderosa pine and grand fir needles.

In Montana's Gallatin National Forest, a wolverine treads a deer path, moving silently over a thick carpet of ponderosa pine and grand fir needles. Following its nose, the wolverine reaches the remains of a moose carcass. Tearing at the carcass is a young grizzly bear that pauses to eye the intruder. The wolverine does not back away. Driven by hunger, it instead charges the bear, which is four times its weight. With a lunge, the wolverine snaps at the bear's nose. The startled bear roars and swipes an enormous paw at the wolverine, but the wolverine is quick to bite at the bear's ears and lips. The bear tries to fight back but is battered by its opponent. The continued harassment is too much for the bear, and it retreats into the forest, leaving the moose carcass to the wolverine, which dives face-first into the moose's shattered ribcage.

WHERE IN THE WORLD THEY LIVE

■ **New World Wolverine**
Canada, Alaska, Rocky
Mountains of western
United States

☐ **Old World Wolverine**
Scandinavia, Siberia

Two wolverine subspecies are found in subarctic and
far northern regions today: the Old World, or Eurasian,
and New World, or North American. Notoriously difficult
to find and observe, wolverines are usually solitary
creatures, and while exact populations are unknown,
they are believed to be most prevalent in the areas as
marked by colored squares on this page.

MYSTERIOUS GLUTTONS

O nce widespread across North America from coast to coast and throughout much of northern Europe and Asia, wolverines are now limited to subarctic regions as well as a few scattered mountainous areas of their former territory. The largest populations of wolverines exist in Scandinavia, Siberia, Canada, and Alaska. While small numbers of wolverines can still be found in the Rocky Mountains of Wyoming, Idaho, and Montana, certain ranges in west-central Montana are home to the greatest number of wolverines in the lower 48 states—perhaps as many as 200 individuals. Wolverines prefer wooded habitats where winters are long and deep snow persists well into May or June.

The wolverine is the third-largest member of the Mustelidae, or weasel, family and the largest land-dwelling mustelid. The 56 members of this family vary greatly in size: the least weasel weighs no more than 9 ounces (255 g), while the giant otter and the sea otter can grow to 70 pounds (31.8 kg) and 100 pounds (45.4 kg) respectively. The wolverine's genus name *Gulo* means "glutton" in Latin and refers to the wolverine's

The fur of the least weasel, a wolverine relative, changes from brown to white in the winter months.

The estimated worldwide population of wolverines is believed to be somewhere between 15,000 and 30,000.

The wolverine's curved claws are so sharp and strong that they enable the animal to climb up sheer cliffs and ice walls.

reputation as a voracious eater. The two subspecies of wolverine are determined by geographical location. Old World wolverines are *Gulo gulo gulo*, while New World wolverines are *Gulo gulo luscus*. Early Europeans gave the wolverine a variety of nicknames, including bear cat, skunk bear, and woods devil. Although wolverines do their best to avoid humans, they have a fearsome reputation amongst people.

Wolverines rarely exceed 45 inches (114.3 cm) from nose to rump and typically weigh from 20 to 45 pounds (9.1–20.4 kg), though males, which weigh about 30 percent more than females, have been found weighing as much as 66 pounds (30 kg). Wolverines have a bushy tail that is 7 to 10 inches (17.8–25.4 cm) long. Their stocky legs measure 10 inches (25.4 cm) long. Despite their relatively bulky size, wolverines are agile and quick. They can run at speeds of up to 15 miles (24.1 km) per hour, turn and roll sharply, and climb trees to chase prey. With five sharply clawed toes widely set on each foot, the wolverine moves as though wearing snowshoes. With its weight evenly distributed, the wolverine is able to walk, and even leap, through deep snow without sinking—an

Despite the shortness of their legs, wolverines are quick and nimble as they track down food sources.

The hairs on a wolverine's tail are each about eight inches (20.3 cm) long, providing protection from cold.

advantage over prey such as caribou and reindeer, which may become trapped in deep snow.

Wolverines and their relatives are mammals. All mammals, with the exceptions of the platypus and echidna, give birth to live offspring and produce milk to feed their young. Mammals are warm-blooded animals. This means that their bodies can work to try to maintain a healthy temperature. Wolverines have a thick coat of **insulating** fur, called pelage, that helps keep them warm. The fur does not absorb water and is so dense that wolverines do not melt snow when they lie down in it. Wolverines vary from brown to nearly black in color, with two light brown or golden stripes running from each shoulder along the side and meeting at the rump. The light-colored fur covers their rounded ears and the upper part of their broad head and also forms a chest mark, called a ventral pattern, which is unique to each wolverine.

While researchers believe that wolverines have only average eyesight and cannot see well past 100 yards (91.4 m), studies have shown that these hunter-scavengers possess a sense of smell so acute that they can detect frozen **carrion** beneath 20 feet (6.1 m) of snow. Wolverines also have excellent hearing, which helps them locate live prey, such as rabbits and rodents, moving beneath snow and brush. Wolverines have one of the strongest bites of all small mammals. Their powerful jaws contain two pairs of long, sharp upper and lower canine teeth and six pairs of pointed incisors at the front of the mouth that are used for ripping flesh. Eight pairs of jagged premolars are used for grinding. The wolverine's unique back teeth—one upper pair and two lower pairs that grow at an angle toward the inside of the mouth—fit together like scissors, giving the wolverine the

The wolverine's one-inch-long (2.5 cm) canine teeth are anchored in its jaw by roots of the same length.

Wolverines can easily overheat, so they spend the summer months high in the mountains where the air is cold.

For reasons not understood by scientists, captive-bred wolverines often do not survive for more than a few weeks.

rare ability to crush and grind thick bones and solidly frozen meat that even grizzly bears would not attempt to eat.

Unlike most of their mustelid relatives, wolverines do not **hibernate**. Because they remain active through the winter, they must seek sustenance wherever possible—and that usually means eating kills made by other predators such as bears, wolves, and cougars. Except for humans, these animals are the wolverine's only natural enemies. An adult wolverine behaves fearlessly toward them and will take on a full-grown bear or cougar—or even a wolf pack—in an attempt to drive the hunter from its kill. Most times, the outcome of such a conflict works in the wolverine's favor.

No meal is too large or too small for a wolverine. Even dried-up bones that appear to be picked clean contain oils and fats that provide nourishment to wolverines, which typically devour every part of the animal—even its teeth. Because wolverines can travel through snow too deep for other predators, they are able to feed on animals killed in falls or by avalanches. By removing dead animals from the **ecosystem**, wolverines provide a valuable service. Wolverines are clever problem-solvers and commonly break into people's storage buildings and cabins to raid

food supplies. They seem to remember which places might contain food and will seek out summer cabins left vacant in winter to search for food.

Wolverines further display their intelligence by recognizing where small mammals hibernate and by planning ahead in hiding food for later consumption. Their seemingly insatiable curiosity keeps wolverines on the move. Clipping along at an average speed of 4 miles (6.4 km) per hour between stops to investigate scents or movements that catch their attention, wolverines typically cover distances of 20 to 40 miles (32.1–64.4 km) a day.

Wolverines often rest in trees, keeping a lookout for prey that may happen to wander by.

Wolverines continue to help their offspring develop hunting and defensive skills for several years.

FAMILY TIES

Little was known about wolverines until recently. Scientists once believed that wolverines were solitary animals, coming together only briefly to mate, but research conducted over the last 10 years has revealed that wolverines have close family relationships that last for many years. Each adult wolverine lives in a particular area called its home range. The size of a male wolverine's home range can reach 500 square miles (1,295 sq km). Females have smaller, separate home ranges that overlap with the home ranges of one or more males.

A male wolverine will not tolerate having unrelated males in his territory. To warn others away, a male urinates or smears musk from his anal glands throughout his home range, a behavior called scent marking. Wolverines travel constantly throughout their territory, marking spots while searching for food. Wolverines even scent mark food that is cached, thus discouraging other animals from eating it.

Wolverines are well known for their trailblazing behavior of never going around obstacles—including the highest peaks in their mountainous territories—and for traveling quickly over terrain so rugged and unforgiving that even the

Snowshoe hares, primary wolverine prey, sport brown fur in the summer and white fur in the winter, providing seasonal camouflage.

Badgers, also members of the weasel family, live in burrows called setts and fiercely defend their territories.

hardiest mountain goats would avoid it. In 2004, researchers with the Wildlife Conservation Society (WCS) tracked a wolverine that traveled more than 550 miles (885 km) in 42 days. Jeff Copeland, one of the world's foremost experts on wolverines, has tracked wolverines climbing over the 10,000-foot (3,048 m) peaks of Idaho's Sawtooth Range.

Because wolverine populations are spread out over vast areas, the mating season is longer, giving the animals time to find each other. From May to August, wolverines call to each other with growls, snarls, and screams. Males are old enough to mate when they are about 2 years old, and females reach maturity by 15 months. Males and females will mate with each other if their home ranges overlap, which means males typically have a number of partners in a mating system called polygyny. A pair of wolverines will spend several days together, mating and feeding, before going their separate ways.

Normal **gestation** for wolverines is only 30 to 50 days, but depending on the time of year a female becomes pregnant, she may put the **embryos** "on hold" for a period of 6 to 8 months. During this time, called embryonic diapause, the female wolverine's fertilized

eggs turn into pinhead-sized balls of cells that float in the **uterus** before developing into baby wolverines, called kits. Such suspension of development ensures that the deep winter snow will have melted by the time the kits are old enough to follow their mother as she hunts and forages for food in spring.

A pregnant wolverine prepares her birthing den before she gives birth (sometime between January and April). She selects an isolated spot at a high elevation—usually under a rock outcropping or the roots of an enormous tree over which deep snow has drifted and air pockets have

A mating pair of wolverines traveling together will share meals without the usual fighting over food.

formed. Sometimes wolverines take over and expand dens abandoned by coyotes or other large animals. The female wolverine digs out a room through which air can flow and lines it with dried vegetation. Then, over two to three days, she gives birth to as many as six kits—though two or three are most common. Some of the kits may have different fathers, ensuring healthy **genetic** diversity of the species.

Wolverine kits are born blind, toothless, and covered in a velvety, pure white fur, which begins to darken after about a week. Newborns weigh only about three ounces (85 g) and are typically no more than five inches (12.7 cm) long. They immediately begin feeding on their mother's milk.

If snowmelt threatens the den's stability, or if other animals discover the den, the mother wolverine will make a new den and move her kits there. In fact, wolverines commonly change dens several times while rearing young. For 9 to 10 weeks, kits are dependent on their mother's milk. Baby wolverines grow quickly, and when they are **weaned**, they begin following their mother as she hunts or scavenges for food. The mother may kill prey such as rodents or fish, leaving the bodies for her kits to find. This helps the kits develop their sense of smell and tracking skills.

The training a wolverine receives during the first year of its life is vital to its survival. In the summer, the father returns to his family to assist the mother in teaching the offspring where to find the best food and how to hunt, cache food, defend themselves, and battle other animals over carrion. Young wolverines are also taught how to steal animals caught in **snares** and traps set by humans— a trait that led Piegan Blackfeet Indians of Montana to call the wolverine "one who steals." A male that mated with several different females travels from family to family, spending time with each one. By mid-September, the juveniles are nearly the size of their mother. They

Young wolverines become responsible for their own meals early in life, so they need good training.

Finding food buried under deep snow is no problem for the wolverine's acute sense of smell.

Fewer than 200 wolverines exist in China, where they struggle with habitat loss, limited food, and illegal hunting.

play-fight with each other and with their parents, travel extensively with their family group, and hunt small prey such as squirrels and rabbits. When winter comes again, the father leaves the family, while the mother and juveniles travel together. The mother may be pregnant again, or she may have chosen to wait a year to mate.

When the next spring comes for the young wolverines, they may wander away to search for their own territories. More often, though, despite being full-grown, they remain with their mother for one more year, during which time their fathers return to visit and continue providing life lessons and training. At about the age of 2, young males are driven away—as far as 200 miles (322 km)—by their fathers to establish their own home ranges, while females are often allowed to set up home ranges near or even overlapping with their mother's. Research conducted by biologists just in the past 10 years has revealed that, even after several generations, mothers and fathers visit the families of their daughters and grandchildren to assist in the training and skill building of the young wolverines—a family bonding practice that is rare among wild animals. In the wild, wolverines typically live 7 to 12 years but may reach the age of 20 in captivity.

Wolverine cubs develop their skills at defensive tactics by play-fighting with each other.

Like other animal species,
young wolverines strengthen
their muscles and increase
their agility through play.

TRICKSTER, MONSTER, HERO

Because wolverines are such secretive animals, most humans know them only by their reputation as fierce predators. For this reason, wolverines have traditionally been associated with ferocity, tenacity, and aggression. While it is true that wolverines demonstrate fearlessness and will rarely back down from a fight— even with animals many times their size—wolverines do not hunt and are not aggressive toward humans unless defending food or their own lives. Nevertheless, wolverines have been traditionally depicted as monsters and demons in the artwork and folklore of many native peoples of North America, Europe, and Russia.

While wolverines are limited to the Arctic and subarctic regions of the globe today, their range was once much larger. Cave paintings dating between 24,000 and 27,000 years old were first discovered in the 19th century in what is now the Czech Republic. Among the many animals depicted on the cave walls at the site, called Predmostí, are wolverines. A wolverine carved out of stone and measuring a little less than two inches (5.1 cm) long was also found at the site. Such carvings,

The USS *Wolverine* was a steamship that ran from 1844 to 1912, and the aircraft carrier USS *Wolverine* served in World War II.

The ice-age-era wolverine pendant from the Eyzies caves is housed at the British Museum in London.

called fetishes, are believed to have been kept as good luck charms, showing the owner's belief in a spiritual connection between humans and animals.

In 2006, at the Eyzies-de-Tayac caves in southwestern France, **archaeologists** discovered the image of a wolverine carved into an elongated, thin slab of bone with a hole in one end—a type of pendant, which may have been worn around the neck on a string of leather. The bone is about 12,500 years old, showing that wolverines existed with humans in Europe during the last ice age. Also in France, La Marche Cave was found to contain nearly 400 slabs of limestone covered with etchings of humans and animals—including wolverines— dating to about 15,000 years ago.

In many North American **cultures**, the wolverine has also been depicted as a trickster—an animal with magical powers and a mischievous or even wicked personality. The **indigenous** Innu people of what is today Canada's northeastern Quebec and western Labrador call the wolverine kuekuatsheu (*KWAY-kwah-choo*). This name was changed by early French fur traders to *carcajou* (*KAR-kuh-joo*), a name by which the wolverine is still called in

parts of Canada. The Innu considered wolverines to be sneaky animals that played tricks on other animals. In a traditional Innu story, Wolverine invites all the ducks and geese to a dance. Loon hears about the dance and wants to come, too. Wolverine tells all the birds to close their eyes as they dance, which they do, but as the music plays, Loon peeks and sees Wolverine choking the birds one by one and piling them up for his supper. Loon calls out, and all the birds fly away. Before Loon can get away, however, Wolverine grabs his tail and pulls out all his tail feathers, which explains why loons have no tail feathers.

The **mythology** of the Plains Cree of Manitoba, Alberta, Saskatchewan, and northern Montana tells of the wolverine-men. It was believed that a person who did truly evil deeds would be transformed into a demon that preyed

The small town of Les Eyzies-de-Tayac-Sireuil is nestled against caves that became a World Heritage site in 1979.

FROM "THE WICKED WOLVERINE"

One day a wolverine was out walking on the hillside, when, on turning a corner, he suddenly saw a large rock.

"Was that you I heard walking about just now?" he asked, for wolverines are cautious animals, and always like to know the reasons of things.

"No, certainly not," answered the rock; "I don't know how to walk."

"But I SAW you walking," continued the wolverine.

"I am afraid that you were not taught to speak the truth," retorted the rock.

"You need not speak like that, for I have SEEN you walking," replied the wolverine, "though I am quite sure that you could never catch ME!" and he ran a little distance and then stopped to see if the rock was pursuing him; but, to his vexation, the rock was still in the same place. Then the wolverine went up close, and struck the rock a blow with his paw, saying: "Well, will you catch me NOW?"

"I can't walk, but I can ROLL," answered the rock.

And the wolverine laughed and said: "Oh, that will do just as well"; and began to run down the side of the mountain.

At first he went quite slowly, "just to give the rock a chance," he thought to himself; but soon he quickened his pace, for he found that the rock was almost at his heels. But the faster the wolverine ran, the faster the rock rolled, and by-and-by the little creature began to get very tired, and was sorry he had not left the rock to itself. . . . At length he grew so weary that he could not even see where he was going, and catching his foot in a branch he tripped and fell. The rock stopped at once, but there came a shriek from the wolverine:

"Get off, get off! Can't you see that you are on my legs?"

"Why did you not leave me alone?" asked the rock. "I did not want to move—I hate moving. But you WOULD have it, and I certainly shan't move now till I am forced to."

by Andrew Lang (1844–1912)

upon his own family. In one story, an old medicine man felt that something bad was going to happen. Day after day he told of his bad feeling, but no one believed him. On the sixth day, the man told the people that a monster was coming—and a monster did come. It was shaped like a wolverine, with short legs and a hunched back, but it was enormous. The people cried and screamed in terror. The old medicine man approached the beast and used his medicine, or magic, to charm the beast into telling him its origin. In life, the beast explained, he had been human, but being a bad human, he was transformed into a giant wolverine with a hunger for human flesh.

Far less gruesome images of wolverines have been used in modern times as symbols of power and tenacity. In the early 20th century, when automobiles were first being manufactured and marketed to the general public, the Wolverine Automobile Company boasted that its 1906 4-cylinder, 4-speed Model E Wolverine could climb hills and reach the impressive speed of 35 miles (56 km) per hour. Its price was $2,000—a hefty sum at that time. From 1927 to 1930, during the age of Prohibition and America's first gangsters, the Reo Motor Car Company also made a model

In 1973, the wolverine was featured on a postage stamp in Mongolia, where the animal is rarely seen today.

Wolverines can be legally trapped in Alaska and Montana, where their water-resistant fur is used to line the hoods of coats.

To keep other animals from finding their hidden food, wolverines urinate on their food caches.

More wolverines are being spotted in northwestern Ontario and Manitoba, where caribou populations have increased since 2007.

called the Wolverine. Both car companies were located in Michigan, which was known as the Wolverine State.

The origin of Michigan's nickname is disputed, but the most popular story is that during a fight over boundaries in 1835, people from Ohio called people from Michigan wolverines because the ornery Michiganders refused to give up the fight for land. Real-life wolverines no longer exist in Michigan, having been overhunted. A lone wolverine spotted in 2004 was the first seen in that state in more than 200 years, but that individual died in 2010. The legacy of the wolverine lives on, and though the state never officially adopted the wolverine as its state symbol, the University of Michigan adopted Wolverines as the name for its sports teams. With nearly 1,000 wins, the Michigan Wolverines have the most all-time victories in college football history.

Perhaps the most famous wolverine comes not from Michigan but from Alaska. A fictional place called Alkali Lake in America's biggest state is where Wolverine, a character in Marvel Comics' X-Men series, was created. The character, whose real name is James "Logan" Howlett, has the sharp senses of a wolverine and the ability to heal almost instantaneously. In a secret laboratory, he was

transformed into a being with a metal-coated skeleton and retractable metal claws, making him virtually indestructible. Upon his first appearance in two 1974 Incredible Hulk comics, Wolverine became a popular character and in 1975 joined the heroic X-Men in their comic series. After appearing in the 20th Century Fox movie *X-Men* (2000) and its sequels, Wolverine became the star of his own series of comics in *Wolverine: Origins* and in movies—*X-Men Origins: Wolverine* (2009) and *The Wolverine* (2013). Though he may not look like a real wolverine, the character exhibits many of the trademark characteristics of this small yet ferocious animal.

Australian actor Hugh Jackman played the character of Wolverine in the X-Men movies of the 2000s.

Reindeer herds in far northern Europe and Russia are under constant threat of wolverine attacks.

PHANTOM OF THE NORTH

In winter, wolverines keep a vigilant eye on prey animals—waiting for them to stumble in deep snow.

An important tradition of the Sami people, who are indigenous to parts of far northern Sweden, Norway, Finland, and Russia, is reindeer herding. About 10,000 of the 70,000 Sami people are known as the *boazovázzi*, or reindeer walkers. Like ranchers in the western United States, the Sami reindeer herders let their livestock roam unattended for part of the year. Wild animals that regularly prey on free-roaming reindeer include wolves, bears, lynx, and wolverines. The Sami believe that wolverines kill reindeer for sport, not for food, because wolverines—considered to be mysterious phantom animals—have been known to attack and kill entire herds over a period of several days or weeks. Wolverines bite the reindeer's leg **tendons** to cripple the reindeer. Then the wolverines bite the reindeer's neck, paralyzing it. The reindeer often docs not die right away, and herders may not find it for several weeks.

Traditionally, the Sami hate wolverines, but since wolverines are protected in many areas of the Arctic, the Sami are not allowed to kill them as they once did. The management of reindeer herds amidst the constant threat of predators has become a serious challenge for the Sami people today. The issue has been addressed by national governments. In fact, one of the goals of the 2000 Convention on the Conservation of European Wildlife and Natural Habitats was to develop and implement strategies to ensure the coexistence of wolverines with humans. The Sami are still waiting for solutions, however.

In North America, wolverines do not pose the same kind of threat as they do in Europe and Russia. Humans affect wolverines more than wolverines affect humans. One example is the use of motorized winter recreational vehicles, such as snowmobiles and ATVs, in wolverine habitats. Such human influence on wolverine behaviors is being investigated in the Payette National Forest of central Idaho by a research team led by Diane Evans Mack, a wildlife biologist with the Idaho Fish & Game Department. The study is co-sponsored by the Idaho State Snowmobile Association. The project was launched in 2009 and continues today. The specific behaviors being studied include wolverine movement and denning habits in areas that are frequently used by people for winter recreation.

To track and study wolverines, these animals must

While wolverines must rest after a heavy meal, they are always ready to run or fight at the hint of a threat.

Wolverines can be hunted in several U.S. states, including Montana, where about 12 are killed each year.

first be captured. Using meat for bait, Mack and her team trap a wolverine in a heavy cage made of logs and designed especially to catch and hold the fearsome animals without harming them. Then a long pole is used to inject the wolverine with a tranquilizer to make it fall asleep. Working quickly, the team fits the wolverine with a collar holding a **Global Positioning System** (GPS) tracking device. Signals sent by the GPS transmitter every 20 minutes allow the biologists to gather precise data on the wolverine's movements. At the same time, GPS devices are used on snowmobiles that are taken into the park, an area spanning some 2 million acres (809,371 ha). By comparing the movements of the wolverines with those of the snowmobiles, researchers will learn if and how the wolverines and humans affect each other.

Conservationists are concerned with the stability of wolverine populations. Since wolverines exist in such large home ranges and must travel great distances to find mates that are not related to them, habitat **fragmentation** could lead to the decline of wolverines in North America. The WCS is also studying ways to avoid or repair habitat fragmentation in the northern Rocky Mountains so

While the wolverine does not live in trees like its cousin the marten, it can climb trees to reach prey such as squirrels.

A wolverine's territory is the same size as a grizzly bear's—but the grizzly is 20 times bigger than the wolverine.

that wolverines can maintain genetic diversity among populations. In 1996, Jeff Copeland, a biologist with the U.S. Forest Service, founded The Wolverine Foundation (TWF) in Idaho to promote interest in wolverine research and conservation. Today, TWF sponsors research projects in the Rocky Mountains, Alaska, Canada, Sweden, and Norway.

One of TWF's ongoing projects in Europe is taking place in and around Sarek National Park, a mountainous region covering roughly 763 square miles (1,977 sq km) in northern Sweden. Most of the nation's wolverines are found in the park, nicknamed "Europe's Last Wilderness." Using log traps, researchers have captured more than

160 wolverines since 2003 and fitted them with radio transmitters. Flying overhead in a small airplane, researchers can track the movements of the wolverines.

In addition to gathering information on population numbers, conservationists are concerned with the genetic health of those populations. A study led by Dr. Audrey Magoun uses camera traps to count and identify wolverines in Alaska. A camera inside a weatherproof box is remotely connected to a device that is tripped when a wolverine approaches a piece of bait hanging from a rope. The idea is to get the wolverine to interact with the bait so that pictures of the animal from various angles can be taken. The pictures clearly identify individual wolverines by their ventral patterns. Magoun has even given her research subjects names. The **DNA** from fur samples collected from baited climbing posts is also helping scientists build a database of wolverines in North America. One of the first study sites was Glacier National Park in Montana, where Jeff Copeland and fellow biologist Rick Yates began the project in 2006.

A man who has dedicated his life to wolverine conservation is Steve Kroschel, who began his career as

In western North America, wolverines keep an eye on herds of Rocky Mountain goats, (above) hoping to eat a fallen goat.

One of Steve Kroschel's rescued wolverine cubs was named Banff (pictured); the other he called Jasper.

Wolverines have been known to consume berries, fruit, and insects in the spring and fall to supplement their diets.

a wildlife filmmaker and now owns Kroschel Wildlife Center in Haines, Alaska. For more than 30 years, Kroschel has studied, filmed, and lived with wolverines. He is one of a handful of people in the world to successfully breed wolverines in the wild and to keep them as tame animals for use in educational programs and documentary films. Kroschel was featured in the 2010 PBS documentary *Wolverine: Chasing the Phantom,* in which he filmed the birth of wolverine twins who then became his lifelong responsibility when their mother died. Pictures of the wolverines, now grown up, can be viewed on his website.

While most of what we know about wolverines has been learned only recently, scientists and conservationists are hopeful that it is not too late to protect wolverines from the effects of human interference, habitat loss, and one of the greatest threats to wolverines: **global warming**. As snowfall levels diminish year after year and spring thaws come earlier, wolverines may face difficulty in rearing young—an activity that requires deep snow cover for many months. Researchers from various nations must come together with common goals and ideas if we are to help the mysterious wolverine survive in our changing world.

When meaty meals are hard to come by, wood-boring insects provide a nutritious, albeit small, snack.

ANIMAL TALE: WHY WOLVERINE LURKS IN THE SHADOWS

Historically, the Passamaquoddy people of what is today Maine and New Brunswick, Canada, spent summers on the Atlantic coast spearfishing and gathering shellfish, but in the winter, they moved inland to trap and hunt game. Like most animal trappers in the north, the Passamaquoddy found wolverines' habit of stealing game from the traps to be aggravating. In this story, the wolverine's personality is revealed.

Long ago, Wolverine was quite handsome. He had the longest legs of all the animals, and his silky fur was a stunning golden color. But Wolverine was conceited. "Oh, what a lovely creature I am," he would often say.

Wolverine, having such long legs, was also quite swift. He challenged Elk to a race, boasting, "I could beat you up one side of the mountain and down the other." And despite Elk's best effort, Wolverine did beat him. Wolverine also challenged Antelope, taunting, "I could beat you down one side of the river valley and up the other." And despite Antelope's tireless struggle, Wolverine did beat him in the race.

Wolverine even challenged Hawk to a race across the meadow, and although Hawk flew straight and swift, Wolverine beat him. Soon, none of the animals would agree to Wolverine's challenges, knowing he would only laugh in their faces when he met them at the finish line.

One day, Snail overheard Wolverine boasting to Rabbit that his golden fur and long legs were much better than Rabbit's. This made Snail angry, for he loved Rabbit, who often dropped bits of sweet herbs for Snail to eat. From the top of a giant boulder, Snail called out, "Hey, Wolverine! I challenge you to a race!"

At this, Rabbit's eyes widened. Wolverine began to laugh. "You?" he snickered. "Why, I could beat you even if you rolled downhill."

"Well then," said Snail, "let's race right here at noon tomorrow."

Wolverine nodded, laughing too hard to speak, and Rabbit dashed off to tell everyone.

At noon the next day, all the animals gathered to watch the race. Bear clapped his paws together to start the race, and Wolverine bolted forward. With great care, Snail tucked himself into a crevice in the giant boulder and gave the old rock a tickle. The boulder began to move, slowly at first, but as it rolled down the hill, it picked up speed.

Hearing a rumbling sound behind him, Wolverine stopped and turned. When he saw the boulder tumbling toward him, he let out a shriek and tried to run, but his long legs got tangled. Down he fell. The boulder rolled right over Wolverine's back and continued down to the bottom of the hill, where it came to rest. Snail crawled out of the crevice, waved to Wolverine, and called, "I believe I have won the race, sir."

Wolverine stood up and shook himself. He tried to run down the hill, but all he could do was lope, for when the boulder had rolled over his back, his long legs had been crushed short. He tried to smooth his coat but found that the fur was ruined.

"You are certainly more clever than I am," Wolverine admitted to Snail. And he loped away in the forest, forever embarrassed by his short legs and rough coat. To this day, Wolverine is seldom seen, hiding in the shadows and raiding traps in the dark.

GLOSSARY

archaeologists – people who study human history by examining ancient peoples and their artifacts

carrion – the rotting flesh of an animal

cultures – particular groups in a society that share behaviors and characteristics that are accepted as normal by that group

DNA – deoxyribonucleic acid; a substance found in every living thing that determines the species and individual characteristics of that thing

ecosystem – a community of organisms that live together in an environment

embryos – unborn or unhatched offspring in the early stages of development

fragmentation – the breaking up of an organism's habitat into scattered sections that may result in difficulty moving safely from one place to another

genetic – relating to genes, the basic physical units of heredity

gestation – the period of time it takes a baby to develop inside its mother's womb

Global Positioning System – a system of satellites, computers, and other electronic devices that work together to determine the location of objects or living things that carry a trackable device

global warming – the gradual increase in Earth's temperature that causes changes in climates, or long-term weather conditions, around the world

hibernate – to spend the winter in a sleeplike state in which breathing and heart rate slow down

indigenous – originating in a particular region or country

insulating – protecting from the loss of heat

mythology – a collection of myths, or popular, traditional beliefs or stories that explain how something came to be or that are associated with a person or object

snares – traps for animals that have a noose made of wire or rope

tendons – tough, inelastic tissues that connect muscle to bone

uterus – the cavity inside a female mammal's body where offspring develop before birth

weaned – to accustom the young of a mammal to take food other than by nursing milk

SELECTED BIBLIOGRAPHY

Chadwick, Douglas. *The Wolverine Way*. Ventura, Calif.: Patagonia, 2012.

National Geographic. "Nat Geo Wild: Wolverine *Gulo gulo*." http://animals.nationalgeographic.com/animals/mammals/wolverine/.

Pontecorvo, Joseph, and Gianna Savoie. *Wolverine: Chasing the Phantom*. DVD. PBS, 2011.

Shaw, Elizabeth Philips, and Jeff Ford. *The Lone Wolverine:*

Tracking Michigan's Most Elusive Animal. Ann Arbor: University of Michigan Press, 2012.

United States Fish & Wildlife Service. "Endangered Species: Wolverine." http://www.fws.gov/mountain-prairie/species/mammals/wolverine/.

Wolverine Foundation. "Kid's Page." http://wolverinefoundation.org/kids-page/.

Note: Every effort has been made to ensure that any websites listed above were active at the time of publication. However, because of the nature of the Internet, it is impossible to guarantee that these sites will remain active indefinitely or that their contents will not be altered.

Although wolverines often elude researchers, persistent study will be important to this animal's future.

INDEX